ALL SORTS
OF
SPORTS TRIVIA
FROM ATLANTIC CANADA

PAUL ARSENEAULT &
PAUL HOLLINGSWORTH

To Scott,
Happy Birthday
& enjoy the book!

NIMBUS
PUBLISHING

Author's note: On December 14, 1991, I lost my older brother Bryce to drug abuse. He was my childhood friend; we shared a bunk bed and a love of sports. My contribution to this book is dedicated in his memory. All financial proceeds to which I am entitled will be donated to teen drug awareness and anti-substance abuse initiatives in Nova Scotia.

—Paul Hollingsworth

Nimbus Publishing Limited
PO Box 9166, Halifax, NS   B3K 5M8
(902) 455-4286

Printed and bound in Canada

Interior design: Reuben Hall
Front cover: John van der Woude
Paul Hollingsworth author photo: Steve Townsend/CTV Atlantic

Library and Archives Canada Cataloguing in Publication
    Arseneault, Paul, 1963-
    All sorts of sports trivia from Atlantic Canada / Paul Arseneault
    and Paul Hollingsworth.
    ISBN 1-55109-587-4

1. Sports—Atlantic Provinces—Miscellanea. 2. Sports—Atlantic
Provinces—History—Miscellanea. I. Hollingsworth, Paul, 1969- II. Title.

GV585.A78 2006   796.09715   C2006-905296-4

We acknowledge the financial support of the Government of Canada through the Book Publishing Industry Development Program (BDIDP) and the Canada Council, and of the Province of Nova Scotia through the Department of Tourism, Culture and Heritage for our publishing activities.

CONTENTS

Preface **v**

Questions **1**

Games **41**

Answers **47**

PREFACE

What is it about sports history and trivia that engages conversation? If you're looking for a meaningful way to pass the time with friends, try bringing up a memorable sports moment. It will be sure to spark broader discussion regarding significant events from previous eras. I call this "good talk"—talk that is sometimes contagious.

Talking about historic, nostalgic or contemporary sporting events—especially when trying to find common ground with someone many years your senior or junior—often proves that we are all bound by cultural ties.

In short, here's my theory: the subject of sports touches the margins of all that matters in our society—current affairs, lifestyle, culture and history. It's not the most important thing—far from it—but isolate a significant image or event from the narrative of our history and sometimes you will find it's also linked to a significant sports event.

This book is called *All Sorts of Sports Trivia*, but if you look closely you'll see it is much more. Yes, it's meant to be entertaining and hopefully challenging, but it's also intended to be a tip of the hat to some of our most outstanding citizens—athletes who worked hard to succeed in life and at the games they played.

Sometimes history tells us a lot about human nature. In this case, by examining Atlantic Canadian sports history we discover a group of heroes who, in some cases, faced stiff competition while also battling poverty, gender bias, and racial discrimination.

Above all else, the questions you are about to read help underscore what I believe to be an irrefutable fact—that sports history in Atlantic Canada is one of the more significant aspects of our cherished culture. There are no NHL, CFL or Major League Baseball teams in our region, but that hardly matters when it comes to honouring the impressive and relevant feats of our strongest competitors.

The recorded accomplishments in this book are not only worthy of historical preservation, they also deserve further discussion, discussion or "good talk" I hope will come from reading this book.

—Paul Hollingsworth

QUESTIONS

1. Fredericton's Willie O'Ree broke the NHL colour barrier in January of 1958. With which one of these "original six" hockey clubs did O'Ree accomplish this historic feat?

   a) Boston Bruins
   b) Chicago Blackhawks
   c) Montreal Canadiens
   d) New York Rangers

2. The Boston Marathon is the most heralded road race in the world, comparable to the Kentucky Derby, Wimbledon or The Masters in terms of prestige. Fred S. Cameron from Advocate Harbour, NS, surprised the sports world when he came out of nowhere to take the event in a time of 2:28:52. In what year did Cameron win the Boston Marathon?

    a) 1890
    b) 1910
    c) 1972
    d) 2003

3. At the World Championship of Rowing in 1867, a Port City quartet shocked Europe by winning the most celebrated regatta in the world. George Price, Robert Fulton, Elijah Ross and Samuel Hutton's defeat of the heavily favoured British and French crews made headlines on both sides of the Atlantic Ocean. What famous moniker did the team take on following their improbable victory?

    a) The Crazy Canucks
    b) The Fearsome Foursome
    c) The Paris Crew
    d) The Fab Four

4. Which of the following Atlantic Canadian cities did not participate in a Stanley Cup final?

    a) Moncton, New Brunswick
    b) Halifax, Nova Scotia
    c) Sydney, Nova Scotia
    d) St. John's, Newfoundland

5. Launched at Lunenburg on March 26, 1921, *Bluenose*, the celebrated schooner from Nova Scotia, raced undefeated for how many consecutive years?

    a) five
    b) ten
    c) fifteen
    d) seventeen

6. Name the Nova Scotia native who was the first black World Boxing Champion.

7. During the 1930s, the top teams in the Maritime Senior Hockey League were known as the Big Four. Name the four teams that formed this league.

8. The Allan Cup is awarded to the Canadian Senior Hockey Champion. Although there are other senior and intermediate hockey trophies, the Allan Cup historically has been the trophy emblematic for amateur hockey success in Canada. Name the first Atlantic Canadian team to win the Allan Cup.

9. What was the "Million Dollar Goal" and which player scored it?

10. For which team did Cole Harbour, NS, native Sidney Crosby make his junior hockey debut?

11. Catchy nicknames are as much a part of a boxer's repertoire as a devastating uppercut or a sharp left hook. Yvon Durelle of Baie St. Anne, NB, was better known as this during his days as a world light heavyweight contender.

    a) The Miramichi Mauler
    b) The Fighting Fisherman
    c) Kid Canuck
    d) The Human Windmill

12. In the 1970s, Frank McKenna, then a young Miramichi lawyer, took on one of the most high-profile sports-related cases in Canada. What was the event that garnered much international attention?

    a) Mr. McKenna defended a Moncton female hockey player's right to play on a boy's midget hockey team.
    b) Mr. McKenna defended Toronto Maple Leafs owner Harold Ballard, who was facing charges of tax evasion.
    c) Mr. McKenna defended Canadian gold medallist Ben Johnson against charges of using performance-enhancing drugs.
    d) Mr. McKenna defended boxer Yvon Durelle against murder charges.

13. Which of these baseball legends spent his summers fishing Atlantic salmon in the world-renowned Miramichi River?

    a) Babe Ruth
    b) Joe DiMaggio
    c) Hank Aaron
    d) Ted Williams

14. Manny McIntyre may not be as well known as some other trailblazers in the world of sport, but his 1946 accomplishment opened the doors for many Canadian athletes. Which of the following feats is attributed to the New Brunswick native?

    a) First wheelchair athlete from New Brunswick to win a medal
    b) First black Canadian to sign a major league baseball contract
    c) First aboriginal to represent Canada at an Olympic Games
    d) First Canadian to sign a professional contract with the British Premier Soccer League

15. Millcove, PEI, native William McIntyre won the first-ever gold medal given out at this international sporting competition.

    a) the Pan Am Games
    b) the Goodwill Games
    c) the Paralympic Winter Games
    d) the British Empire Games

16. In 1952, Nova Scotian Danny Gallivan began a thirty-two-year career with the Montreal Canadiens as the team's TV and radio play-by-play announcer. Gallivan would go on to call more than 1,800 NHL games. Before joining Montreal, Gallivan was a radio play-by-play man in Halifax. For which team did he work as an announcer?

17. Name the hockey player from Nova Scotia who once scored three goals in a six-second span during a university hockey game.

18. From 1946–59, the Halifax and District Baseball League featured semi-pro and future major league stars from Canada and the United States. Name the former Truro Bearcat who went on to set World Series records for strikeouts by a relief pitcher and consecutive strikeouts by a pitcher in a single game.

19. Name the long distance runner from Nova Scotia who won the Boston Marathon twice.

20. Name the former Dartmouth Arrows (of the Halifax and District Baseball League) first baseman/outfielder who would later be an original member of the expansion Montreal Expos.

21. What was the name of the Dartmouth baseball field at which the Arrows played during the Halifax and Dartmouth League baseball era?

22. Halifax, NS, native Wendell Young won back-to-back Stanley Cups with which of these NHL champions?

    a) New York Islanders (1981–82, 1982–83)
    b) Edmonton Oilers (1986–87, 1987–88)
    c) Pittsburgh Penguins (1990–91, 1991–92)
    d) Detroit Red Wings (1996–97, 1997–98)

23. New Brunswick Senior Baseball League graduate Matt Stairs is one of Canada's most accomplished professional athletes. Which of the following statements applies to the Fredericton, NB, native?

   a) Stairs is the first major league baseball player ever to hit the baseball out of Fenway Park.
   b) Stairs is one of only two Canadians to hit thirty-five or more home runs in a single season.
   c) Stairs is the first Canadian to hit for the cycle (home run, triple, double, single in the same game).
   d) Stairs is the first Canadian to be named captain of a Major League Baseball club (Oakland Athletics, 1999).

24. Gerard Gallant of Summerside, PEI, and all-world centreman Steve Yzerman were one of the most prolific scoring tandems in professional hockey in the 1980s and early 1990s. Gallant is now a member of the NHL coaching fraternity as the head coach of which franchise?

   a) St. Louis Blues
   b) Columbus Blue Jackets
   c) Chicago Blackhawks
   d) Washington Capitals

25. CFL running back Eric Lapointe was awarded the Hec Creighton Trophy for most outstanding football player in the CIS in both 1996 and 1998. Which of these clubs had the Montreal native in its backfield?

   a) Mount Allison Mounties
   b) Saint Mary's Huskies
   c) Acadia Axemen
   d) St. Francis Xavier X-Men

26. Newfoundland's Bob Cole is now known as the voice of *Hockey Night in Canada*. This long-time hockey broadcaster is also a pretty fair athlete, having participated in one of the following national championships in 1971 and 1975.

    a) The Vanier Cup (college football)
    b) The Bell Canadian Open (golf)
    c) The Brier (curling)
    d) The Memorial Cup (junior hockey)

27. Name the Halifax native who was the first Canadian boxer to win a gold medal at the Pan Am Games.

28. In 1996, the Winnipeg Jets transferred their hockey operations to Phoenix where they became the Coyotes. One person has served as head coach in both Phoenix and Winnipeg. Name him.

29. The WP McGee Trophy is awarded to the Canadian Interuniversity Sport (CIS) Men's Basketball Champion. What three Maritime university teams have won the national championship?

30. Through 2005, there have only been two Maritime-born NHL players to win the Conn Smythe trophy as the Most Valuable Player throughout the Stanley Cup playoffs. Name the players, the years they won the award, and the teams they played for.

31. In the history of Canadian Interuniversity Sport (CIS), there has been only one Nova Scotia-born head football coach. Name him.

32. Shediac's Gordie Gallant was one of the toughest hombres ever to play in the World Hockey Association. Best remembered for his time as a Minnesota Fighting Saint, Gallant earned coin tangling with such legendary enforcers as Dave Hanson, "Cowboy" Bill Flett and the legendary Steve "Missing Link" Durbano. In 1972, Gallant rode shotgun in the North Shore Hockey League. Which northern New Brunswick franchise did Gallant play for?

    a) Chatham Ironmen
    b) Campbellton Tigers
    c) Bathurst Papermakers
    d) Dalhousie Rangers

33. Rob Butler of Conception Bay, NL, sports a World Series ring courtesy of which MLB club?

    a) 1990 Cincinnati Reds
    b) 1993 Toronto Blue Jays
    c) 1995 Atlanta Braves
    d) 1999 New York Yankees

34. A Moncton teacher was selected to be the very first captain of the Canadian Olympic women's hockey team. Can you guess the name of that honoured athlete from the following list of team members?

    a) Stacey Wilson
    b) Cassie Campbell
    c) Leslie Reddon
    d) Therese Brisson

35. Chris Skinner of St. John's, NL, was a powerful running back who combined grit and grace during his eight-year CFL career. Skinner, a Bishop's Gator all-star during his college career, won one Grey Cup during his tenure. With which team did he win it?

    a) Montreal Concordes
    b) Ottawa Roughriders
    c) Calgary Stampeders
    d) Edmonton Eskimos

36. In 1986, four short years after leading this CIS hockey powerhouse to back-to-back national championships, Jean Perron helped the Habs win the holy grail of hockey with a five-game triumph over the Calgary Flames. Which of the following university clubs did Perron lead to consecutive national titles?

    a) UPEI Panthers
    b) Saint Mary's Huskies
    c) Dalhousie Tigers
    d) Moncton Blue Eagles

37. Since 1965, the Vanier Cup has been awarded to the football champions in Canadian university sport. Name the Maritime schools that have won the championship and the years they accomplished the feat.

38. Through 2006, only three Nova Scotia hockey players have won a gold medal at the IIHF World Junior Hockey Championship. Name the players and the years they won gold.

39. Name the two Maritime cities to play host to exhibition games in the Canadian Football League.

40. The American Hockey League's PEI Senators had a brief Charlottetown-based existence from 1993–1996. Who was the Senators' head coach during their inaugural season?

41. In the history of the Olympic Summer Games, only two Atlantic Canadian boxers have won boxing medals. Name the boxers and the years they medalled.

42. Each year the CBC selects a town to host the wildly popular *Hockey Day in Canada*. Which of the following regional hockey hotbeds was given that honour in 2006?

    a) Montague, PEI
    b) St. Stephen, NB
    c) Stephenville, NL
    d) Amherst, NS

43. The Uteck Bowl is a CIS football championship named after long-time Saint Mary's Huskies head coach Larry Uteck. The former Saint Mary's Athletic Director led the Huskies to three Vanier Cup appearances during his head coaching tenure. A decorated CFL All-Star, Uteck also helped which of these Canadian Football League clubs to a Grey Cup appearance in 1978?

    a) Edmonton Eskimos
    b) BC Lions
    c) Winnipeg Blue Bombers
    d) Montreal Alouettes

44. Fifty goals in a single season is one of the most sought-after achievements in the NHL. Which of the following Atlantic Canadian hockey players has attained the half-century mark?

a) Dan Cleary
b) Danny Grant
c) Brad Richards
d) Gordie Drillon

45. Canada's Charline Labonté spent some quality time in the Quebec Major Junior Hockey League before leading her country to a gold medal in the 2006 Torino Olympics. Which of the following teams did the Boisbriand, QC, product tend goal for?

a) Cape Breton Screaming Eagles
b) Halifax Mooseheads
c) PEI Rocket
d) Acadie-Bathurst Titan

46. Chatham Ironmen ace Jason Dickson was a major league all-star in 1997. Dickson had a 13–9 record and was the lone representative for his team during that year's mid-season classic. Which team did Dickson represent at the All-Star game?

a) Anaheim Angels
b) Montreal Expos
c) Toronto Blue Jays
d) St. Louis Cardinals

47. Former St. Louis, Montreal, Buffalo, Pittsburgh and Detroit head coach Scotty Bowman is hockey's all-time leader in wins by a professional head coach with 1,244. Who is second?

48. Name the only Nova Scotian to play for Canada's women's volleyball team at the summer Olympics.

49. In 2005–2006, there were four players in the NHL who were also former players in the Maritime Junior 'A' Hockey League. Name them.

50. Moncton was home to four American Hockey League franchises from 1978–1993. During the AHL era in the Hub City, only one player scored fifty goals in a single season. Who was it and when did he do it?

51. Who is the only Newfoundland skip to win the Brier?

52. Summerside, PEI, has gained a reputation as a wonderful special events host. The town has shown the ability to successfully host provincial, national and international events whether they be in softball, soccer or hockey. In September of 2002, the island community welcomed an NHL team for its pre-season camp; can you guess which pro franchise called Summerside home in the fall of '02?

    a) Montreal Canadiens
    b) Columbus Blue Jackets
    c) Carolina Hurricanes
    d) Toronto Maple Leafs

53. Former Moncton Met moundsman Rheal Cormier has been one of the more reliable left-handed pitchers in pro baseball over the past decade. Cormier, who debuted as a starter in the 1991 season, has adjusted very well to his latest role as a middle reliever and set-up man. Which one of these clubs has not had Cormier as part of its pitching staff?

    a) St. Louis Cardinals
    b) Philadelphia Phillies
    c) Tampa Bay Devil Rays
    d) Boston Red Sox

54. The pride of Kensington, PEI, Anna Pendergast-Stammberger was a fixture on Canada's national basketball team in the early to mid-eighties. In 1984, Pendergast-Stammberger accomplished something never done by a female athlete from PEI. What was it?

    a) Her bronze medal performance in the Los Angeles Olympics in 1984 was the first ever for a female athlete from PEI.
    b) Her participation in the LA Games was the first ever for a female athlete from PEI.
    c) At forty years old, Pendergast-Stammberger became the oldest female athlete from PEI to participate in an Olympic Games.
    d) At seventeen, Pendergast-Stammberger was the youngest female athlete from PEI to participate in an Olympic Games.

55. Everett Sanipass of Big Cove, NB, was a first-round pick in the NHL draft of 1986. Which of these original six entries made the Verdun product their fourteenth pick overall?

    a) Chicago Blackhawks
    b) New York Rangers
    c) Boston Bruins
    d) Detroit Red Wings

56. Drafted first overall by the Pittsburgh Penguins in July of 2005, against which team did Sidney Crosby make his NHL regular season debut?

57. From 1981–1986, Halifax's Robbie Forbes won major scoring titles in all four Atlantic Canadian provinces. Names the years, teams, and leagues.

58. Name the curler who holds the record for most Scott Tournament of Hearts championships.

59. Name the only four NHL players from Nova Scotia to score one hundred points or more during an NHL regular season.

60. Who is the only Nova Scotia-born head coach of a Stanley Cup winning hockey team?

61. The Toronto Maple Leafs have twice been affiliated with Atlantic Canada-based American Hockey League franchises. Name the farm teams.

62. U.S. President Bill Clinton made history in 1998 by becoming the first sitting president to take in an NHL playoff game. Which of the following NB pucksters participated in that game?

    a) John Leblanc
    b) Kent Paynter
    c) Scott Fraser
    d) Mike Eagles

63. The 2004 Canadian Olympic women's softball team may have been one of the strongest in the history of the program. An offensive dynamo from Irishtown, NB, was an important cog in Team Canada's entry in the Athens Games. Can you identify her?

    a) Hayley Wickenheiser
    b) Vicky Bastarache
    c) Janiva Willis
    d) Sandy Newsham

64. Arguably New Brunswick's greatest-ever Olympic athlete, three-time Olympian Marianne Limpert of Fredericton was a mainstay on Canada's Olympic swimming team in the 1990s. At the 1996 Olympics in Atlanta, Marianne finished second to the controversial Michelle Smith of Ireland. In what discipline did Limpert win her silver medal?

    a) 100 metre butterfly
    b) 200 metre butterfly
    c) 200 metre individual medley
    d) 800 metre freestyle

65. In 1981, Dartmouth native Rob McCall and his ice dance partner Marie McNeil finished first at the Canadian Figure Skating Championship. The next season, McCall and his new ice dance partner, Tracy Wilson, began a streak of seven consecutive first place finishes at the Canadian Championships. The tandem of Wilson and McCall also captured one Olympic medal for Canada. Which of the following statements is correct?

    a) Wilson and McCall won a silver medal at the 1980 Lake Placid Winter Olympics.
    b) Wilson and McCall won a gold medal at the 1984 Sarajevo Winter Olympics.
    c) Wilson and McCall won a bronze medal at the 1988 Calgary Winter Olympics.
    d) Wilson and McCall won a gold medal at the 1988 Calgary Winter Olympics.

66. Fredericton's Therese Brisson is widely regarded as the first superstar of women's hockey. Brisson's game has often been described as intelligent and cerebral; that would make sense considering she once was a professor at this Atlantic Canadian institution of higher learning.

    a) Acadia University
    b) St. Thomas University
    c) Université de Moncton
    d) University of New Brunswick

67. In the 1980s, five Cape Breton natives won Stanley Cups. Name each winner, the year they did it, and with which team.

68. Name the first-ever Cape Breton native to work as an on-ice official in the National Hockey League.

69. The Hec Creighton award goes to the most outstanding football player in Canadian Interuniversity Sport. The award has gone to players from the Atlantic Conference five times. Name the players, their teams, and the years they captured the trophy.

70. Since 1971, the Centennial Cup/Royal Bank Cup (the championship was renamed in 1996) has been awarded to the Canadian Junior 'A' Hockey Champion. Two Maritime teams have won this national championship. Name the team and the years they won.

71. The first Canada Winter Games were held in 1967 at Quebec City. Two years later, in 1969, the first Canada Summer Games were held in the Maritimes. What cities played host to the 1969 Canada Summer Games?

72. Which of the following Atlantic Canadians has played over 1,000 NHL games?

   a) Errol Thompson
   b) Don Sweeney
   c) Charlie Bourgeois
   d) Keith Brown

73. Paul Hodgson of Fredericton, NB, was a rising star in the Toronto Blue Jays system when injuries forced the outfielder to quit the game in 1980. Hodgson's post-MLB career also thrust him into the public spotlight. Which of the following statements is correct?

    a) Paul Hodgson became a Liberal MLA for Fredericton from 1987 to 1991.
    b) Paul Hodgson became a broadcaster for the CBC.
    c) Paul Hodgson landed a role in the CBC hit show *Street Legal*.
    d) Paul Hodgson was elected Fredericton's twenty-fifth mayor on May 14, 1986.

74. Clarence Bastarache of Bouctouche, NB, represented wheelchair athletes with pride when he won a gold medal at the 1973 Pan American Wheelchair Games. In what sport did Bastarache win his gold medal at these Lima, Peru, games?

    a) basketball
    b) javelin
    c) pentathlon
    d) discus

75. Which of the following Atlantic Canadian provinces is the only one ever to medal at the Esso National Women's Hockey Championships?

    a) Nova Scotia
    b) New Brunswick
    c) Prince Edward Island
    d) Newfoundland

76. Ron Turcotte of Grand Falls, NB, won the 1973 Triple Crown with the horse that is widely regarded as the greatest racer ever. What was the name of the horse that Turcotte rode while winning that year's Kentucky Derby, Belmont Stakes, and Preakness?

   a) Seattle Slew
   b) Affirmed
   c) Citation
   d) Secretariat

77. From 1971 to 2005, the American Hockey League had teams playing in seven Atlantic Canadian cities under various NHL affiliations. During that time six teams from the Atlantic region won championships. Name the teams and years that Atlantic Canadian AHL franchises captured the Calder Cup awarded to league champions.

78. Name the two major league baseball players who played for Team Canada both at the 1988 Summer Olympics and the 2006 World Baseball Classic.

79. In 1972 the Nova Scotia Voyageurs became the first Atlantic Canadian-based team in the American Hockey League. The AHL would stay in Halifax for the next twenty-two years. Name the five NHL franchises to have affiliation with Halifax-based AHL teams.

80. In 1994 the Halifax Mooseheads were the first Atlantic Canadian-based Quebec Major Junior Hockey League franchise. Name the second Atlantic Canadian-based QMJHL team.

81. Name the only New Brunswick skip to win the Canadian Women's Curling Championship.

82. Which of the following Nova Scotian universities has made the most appearances at the CIS Women's National Hockey Championships?

    a) University College of Cape Breton (now University of Cape Breton)
    b) Dalhousie University
    c) St. Francis Xavier University
    d) Saint Mary's University

83. In March of 2006, Joyce Slipp, a legend in university athletics, announced her retirement as a head coach at UNB. In 1976, Slipp was given the tremendous honour of being named captain of one of our Olympic teams. Can you correctly guess the team she led at the Summer Games in Montreal?

    a) national basketball team
    b) national volleyball team
    c) national field hockey team
    d) national water polo team

84. Darren Ritchie of Saint John, NB, shocked the nation by winning the 1992 Canadian Amateur Golf Championship. Which of these famous PGA members ended up in second place, two shots behind the upstart from the port city?

    a) Mike Weir
    b) Stephen Ames
    c) Ernie Els
    d) Phil Mickelson

85. In the mid-1980s, softball was extremely popular on the Atlantic Canada sports scene. Which of the following Atlantic Canada-based provincial entries captured the National Women's Softball Championship in 1984?

    a) Team Newfoundland
    b) Team New Brunswick
    c) Team Prince Edward Island
    d) Team Nova Scotia

86. Originally from Midland, ON, Moncton's Russ Howard won a gold medal at the Torino Olympics of 2006 as the elder statesman on the Brad Gushue rink. What position did Russ ultimately assume with his new team?

    a) skip
    b) second
    c) third
    d) fourth

87. Since 1950, the Alexander Cup has gone to eastern Canadian Major Senior Hockey Champions from various leagues. Name the two Maritime teams to win the Alexander Cup.

88. Newfoundland has had just one athlete or team from the province win an Olympic medal. Who won, when was the medal won, and in which competition?

89. Which of the following statements is true?

   a) Sidney Crosby, Al MacInnis and Brad Richards have all won a Memorial Cup.
   b) Sidney Crosby, Al MacInnis and Brad Richards have all won the Conn Smythe Trophy.
   c) Sidney Crosby, Al MacInnis and Brad Richards have all played for the Rimouski Oceanic.
   d) Sidney Crosby, Al MacInnis and Brad Richards have all scored 100 points in a single NHL season.
   e) None of the above.

90. In addition to Colleen Jones, one other Nova Scotia skip has won the Scott Tournament of Hearts. Name the curler and the year she won.

91. Name the Nova Scotia swimmer who won two bronze medals for Canada at the 1976 Summer Olympics in Montreal.

92. The Air Canada Cup (in 2005 renamed the Telus Cup) goes to the Canadian Major Midget AAA Champion. Which of the following hockey teams has won the Air Canada/Telus Cup?

   a) Halifax McDonalds
   b) Dartmouth Subways
   c) St. John's Midget AAA Maple Leafs
   d) Fredericton Midget AAA Canadiens
   e) None of the above

93. Bathurst's Elizabeth Bouma was team leader for our national figure skating team during the 2002 Salt Lake City Olympics. In what international controversy did Bouma find herself a major player during her time in Utah?

    a) A betting scandal that involved members of the International Skating Federation.
    b) An officiating scandal that initially robbed Canadians Jamie Salé and David Pelletier of their gold medal.
    c) A doping scandal that disqualified two Team Canada skaters.
    d) Two members of China's figure skating team sought asylum with Team Canada.

94. You might love him or you might hate him, but no one can deny the value of Moncton's charismatic René Duprée to the WWE RAW brand. In 2003, Duprée teamed up with fellow Canadian Sylvain Grenier to form which one of the following tag teams?

    a) The Natural Disasters
    b) La Résistance
    c) Les Voltigeurs
    d) The Royal Canadian Mounted Police

95. In November of 2002, a New Brunswick hockey dad made national headlines after he sued the provincial amateur hockey association. Why did Micheal Croteau seek damages from Hockey NB?

    a) His son was suspended for forty games for hitting another player from behind.
    b) His thirteen-year-old son was banned from playing junior hockey due to age restrictions.
    c) His son was not awarded the league's MVP award.
    d) His son was suspended for a year for pushing an official.

96. Prince Edward Island has been selected to host the 2009 Canada Summer Games. The Island, which has gained a reputation for hosting premier national and international sporting events, will be hosting the event for the second time. Which of the following Games was also hosted by Prince Edward Island?

    a) 1985 Canada Summer Games
    b) 1991 Canada Winter Games
    c) 2001 Canada Summer Games
    d) 2003 Canada Winter Games

97. Name the Nova Scotian who, as a head coach, won a Stanley Cup one year in the National Hockey League, only to be demoted to the American Hockey League and then coach his new team to a Calder Cup Championship the following season?

98. Who is the only Nova Scotia canoeist to win an Olympic medal?

99. What Fredericton, NB, native was named NHL Rookie of the Year in 1969?

100. Name the first and only Maritime team to win the Canadian Senior Football Championship.

101. On February 13, 1999, the Toronto Maple Leafs played their final game at Maple Leaf Gardens before moving to the brand new Air Canada Centre. What Nova Scotia native sang "The Maple Leaf Forever" as part of the official closing ceremonies?

102. Jeff "The Terminator" Reardon was once the most intimidating reliever in all of major league baseball. Reardon was lights out in 1987 as he led his Minnesota Twins to an exciting seven-game World Series win over St. Louis. The former Saint John Dodger made a different sort of headline in December 2005, however. Can you guess the story now associated with this former NB Senior League pitcher?

  a) Reardon was arrested on charges of armed robbery.
  b) Reardon was banned for life for gambling on baseball during his playing days.
  c) Reardon was fired as manager of the San Diego Padres.
  d) Reardon was implicated in the Barry Bonds doping scandal.

103. Prince Edward Island's Lori Kane is an inspiration to every female golfer in Canada. A two-time winner of the Bobbie Rosenfeld Award for the top female athlete in the nation, Kane has earned over six million dollars and continues to be a force on the LPGA a decade into her pro career. In what year did Kane win her first LPGA tournament?

    a) 1996
    b) 1998
    c) 2000
    d) 2002

104. Which of these Atlantic Canadian recording artists brought down the house as the headline act at the 2001 NHL All-Star game in Denver, Colorado?

    a) The Rankins
    b) Great Big Sea
    c) Roch Voisine
    d) Sloan

105. What circumstance conspired to deny any Atlantic Canadians the chance to participate in the 1980 Summer Games in Moscow?

    a) The Olympic Games were cancelled in 1980 for security reasons.
    b) Canada joined a list of nations that decided to boycott the 1980 Olympic Games.
    c) No Atlantic Canadian athletes qualified for the Olympic Games in 1980.
    d) The 1980 Olympics were cancelled after only one day due to an outbreak of influenza.

106. In March of 2004, Frederic Niemeyer of Restigouche County, NB, was ranked #134 in the world in this sport.

    a) light heavyweight boxing
    b) ping pong
    c) ballroom dancing
    d) tennis

107. In 2006, the Moncton Wildcats hosted the Memorial Cup, emblematic of major junior hockey supremacy in North America. The Wildcats were the second Maritime-based Major Junior Hockey franchise to host the tournament. What franchise was the first to host the Memorial Cup round robin tournament?

108. Name the curling skip who has won two men's World Curling Championships but has never won a Brier while representing his current home province of New Brunswick.

109. Who is the youngest player in the history of the National Hockey League to score 100 points in a single season?

110. In 1980–81, the Atlanta Flames moved their hockey operations to Calgary. What Nova Scotian was the first-ever head coach for the Calgary Flames?

111. Name the only Nova Scotia-born rower to win a medal in Olympic competition.

112. The most entertaining pro ball player ever to play the game may have been Boston Red Sox legend Bill "Spaceman" Lee. Lee's take on life generated more notable quotes than any other athlete in recent history. In 1984, Lee took his still-lethal left arm to the New Brunswick Senior Baseball League. Can you guess the team that landed the "Spaceman"?

    a) Bathurst Thunderbirds
    b) Newcastle Cardinals
    c) Woodstock Shiretowners
    d) Moncton Mets

113. The supremely talented Steve Nash has won his second NBA MVP award. The Victoria, BC, point guard has a direct connection to St. Francis Xavier University. Can you identify it from the list below?

    a) Nash played one year for St. F. X. (1992–1993) before moving south to Santa Clara University.
    b) Steve's brother Brad was a point guard for the X-Men during the late eighties.
    c) St. F. X. bench boss Steve Konchalski coached Nash at the 1996 Tournament of the Americas.
    d) Nash's three-point buzzer beater gave his UVic team a gold medal victory over St. F. X. at the 1993 CIS Men's Basketball Championships.

114. Prince Edward Island celebrated a world curling championship in 2001 when Suzanne Gaudet skipped Canada's rink to a gold medal in the World Junior Curling Championship final. Whom did Gaudet beat to bring the maple leaf the junior gold in 2001?

    a) Team USA
    b) Team Sweden
    c) Team Switzerland
    d) Team Japan

115. Which of the following CIS entries has won a Canadian Men's National Soccer Championship?

    a) St. Thomas University
    b) Memorial University
    c) University College of Cape Breton (now University of Cape Breton)
    d) University of New Brunswick

116. Milaine Theriault won her first national championship medal in 1992 and was a key member of Team Canada's entry at the Nagano Olympics in 1998, Salt Lake City in 2002 and Torino in 2006. Can you guess what sport the accomplished athlete from St. Quentin, NB, excelled in?

    a) luge
    b) figure skating
    c) Nordic skiing
    d) women's hockey

117. The Jack Adams Award is given to the top head coach in the National Hockey League. Name the Jack Adams winner who in 2005–2006 coached a Maritime-based QMJHL team after winning the NHL Coach of the Year Award.

118. On July 21, 1981, Halifax boxer Trevor Berbick captured the Commonwealth Heavyweight Boxing Championship at the Halifax Metro Centre. Whom did Berbick defeat to win the title?

119. Name the Sydney, NS, native who in 1968–69 finished second to Danny Grant in balloting for the NHL's Rookie of the Year Award.

120. On April 29, 1980, Chris Clarke beat a Halifax boxer to capture the Canadian Middleweight Championship, only to be knocked out by the same fighter in a rematch five months later. Who was Clarke's opponent?

121. In addition to the Moncton Hawks and Halifax Wolverines teams from the 1930s, four other Atlantic Canadian teams have also captured the Allan Cup. Name the teams and the years they captured the trophy.

122. In what year did Fredericton's Jim Sullivan win the World Junior Curling Championship?

    a) 1940
    b) 1968
    c) 1988
    d) 2001

123. This two-time Olympian from Caraquet, NB, was at one point the third ranked attacker in the World Volleyball League. A tremendous hitter, he won a starting job for Team Canada at the 1992 Barcelona Olympics after having captured the MVP trophy in that year's Olympic qualifying tournament. Can you name this decorated international athlete?

    a) Oscar Gaudet
    b) J. P. Dumont
    c) Marc Albert
    d) Pierre Pilote

124. Leroy Washburn of Oromocto, NB, won the 1974 New Brunswick Track and Field Championships, officiated track and field at the 1976 Summer Olympics in Montreal, and served as a chef de mission at the 1987 World Student Games. In what category did Washburn enter the New Brunswick Sports Hall of Fame in 1988?

    a) athlete
    b) builder
    c) official
    d) team

125. When one thinks of auto racing in our country, Paul Tracy and the father–son team of Gilles and Jacques Villeneuve immediately come to mind, but it was a Prince Edward Island racer who made Canadian racing history with a victory at the 90,000 seat Pomona Raceway in February of 1970. In which of the following categories of racing did Barry Poole make history?

    a) Formula One
    b) Super Stock
    c) Nascar
    d) Off Road

126. Summerside, PEI's Carol Moore-Fitzsimmons has been an elite athlete since the age of ten when she represented her province at the Canada Winter Games. The child prodigy would move on to represent her nation in the early 1980s and wrap up her career with a winning performance at the 1994 Master's World Championships in Montreal. What sport did Moore-Fitzsimmons excel at?

    a) synchronized swimming
    b) rhythmic gymnastics
    c) Nordic skiing
    d) figure skating

127. A draft pick of the Montreal Canadiens in 1982, Troy Crosby, father of Sidney, played two seasons in the Quebec Major Junior Hockey League. For which QMJHL team did the goalie play?

128. Name the hockey player who in 1970–71 was named Rookie of the Year in the now defunct Maritime Junior Hockey League, and who returned nineteen years later as the head coach of the AHL's Halifax Citadels.

129. On April 7, 2006, what NHL referee and Nova Scotia native worked his 1500th regular season game?

130. Since the QMJHL expanded to the Maritimes in 1994, three Maritime-based teams have played in the Memorial Cup tournament. Name the teams.

131. Since the 1962–63 season, the University Cup has been awarded annually to the Canadian Interuniversity Sport Men's Hockey Champion. Of all the teams that have competed in the play-downs for the trophy, the Calgary Dinos have made ten appearances without winning a national title. What Maritime university hockey team is second to Calgary for most University Cup tournament appearances without winning the national title?

132. Lise Gautreau-Robichaud of Moncton was a Canadian Junior Champion in rhythmic gymnastics in 1981 and 1982, and an Eastern Canadian Champion from 1980–82 and again in 1984. Despite her dominance in the sport in Canada in the 1980s, Gautreau attended only one Olympic Games; which one was it?

   a) 1980 (Moscow)
   b) 1984 (Los Angeles)
   c) 1988 (Seoul)
   d) 1992 (Barcelona)

133. In which sport did Edmundston's Shawn Sawyer participate at the 2006 Torino Olympics?

    a) figure skating
    b) curling
    c) biathlon
    d) luge

134. Which of these World Wrestling Federation legends spent
much time training in and around the railway yards in Moncton, NB?

    a) "Rowdy" Roddy Piper
    b) Hulk Hogan
    c) Bobby "The Brain " Heenan
    d) André the Giant

135. Saint John's Mark Lackie won a silver medal at the 1992
Winter Olympic Games in Albertville, France, in which of the
following sports?

    a) speed skating
    b) figure skating
    c) downhill skiing
    d) snowboarding

136. In 1998, at the Nagano Olympic Games, PEI's Dave "Eli" MacEachern became embroiled in one of the more bizarre happenings in the annals of competitive bobsleigh. Can you identify the event that MacEachern and his Team Canada partner Pierre Lueders were involved in?

    a) Team Germany was disqualified for trying to sabotage the Canadian team's sleigh.
    b) Team Canada and Team Italy would share the gold medal after posting identical times.
    c) Team Canada and Team USA refused to race at Nagano due to dangerous track conditions.
    d) Team Canada was given the gold after being the only team to finish the demanding course.

137. This East Riverside, NB, athlete was a pioneer in the sport of snowboarding. Ranked in the top five internationally in his sport throughout the nineties, he was named the Alpine Rider of the Year by *Ski Racing* magazine in 1997 and was a member of Canada's delegation at Nagano during the sport's inaugural appearance at the Olympic games. Who is he?

    a) Ross Rebagliati
    b) Mike Michalchuk
    c) Jasey Jay Anderson
    d) Mark Fawcett

138. Recently, Julian, Ricky and Bubbles of the *Trailer Park Boys* appeared in a Tragically Hip music video along with this Canadian sports icon:

    a) Don Cherry
    b) Cindy Klassen
    c) Steve Nash
    d) Mark Messier

139. Which of the following Atlantic Canadian destinations plays host to the World Pond Hockey Championships?

  a) Montague, PEI
  b) Gander, NL
  c) Glace Bay, NS
  d) Plaster Rock, NB

140. Who was the last head coach for the Nova Scotia Voyageurs?

141, In the three seasons leading into his rookie NHL season (from 2002–2005), Sidney Crosby played for which seven teams?

142. What is Sidney Crosby's nickname?

143. Through 2006, Nova Scotia has captured the Canadian Men's Curling Championship three times. Name the three Nova Scotia skips to win the Brier and the years in which they captured the title.

144. Perhaps the biggest surprise of the 2003 NBA draft centered around the player who did not get drafted. Newfoundland's Carl English was thought to be a solid second-round pick heading into the lottery, but was shocked and saddened to find himself still undrafted as the final selection came and went. What university did English attend during his stay in the NCAA?

a) Duke
b) Kentucky
c) Hawaii
d) Gonzaga

145. Name the only Nova Scotia-born hockey player to be named captain for Canada's Men's Olympic hockey team.

146. In 2002 the Halifax Forum celebrated its seventy-fifth anniversary. When it first opened in 1927, the forum featured the only artificial ice-making machine east of Montreal. Which teams played the first-ever hockey game at the forum?

147. In 1991, the Metro Valley Junior 'A' Hockey League was renamed the Maritime Junior 'A' Hockey League, mainly because the league had expanded beyond the Metro-Halifax and Annapolis Valley regions. Name the first-ever non-Nova Scotia team admitted into the Metro Valley League.

148. Name the Maritime city that played host to the first-ever Centennial Cup.

149. William D. (Bill) Mackinnon's sports resume ranks with any amateur athlete in Canada. Mackinnon, a UPEI alumnus, was a gold medal winner at the 1969 Canada Games. In addition to representing his home province in 1969, Mackinnon represented his country as a member of the national junior team and Pan Pacific Games team. In which of the following sports did Mackinnon make his mark?

    a) swimming
    b) cycling
    c) track and field
    d) rowing

150. In the 1985–1986 season, a player from Oromocto, NB, led the American Hockey League's Fredericton Express in scoring. Can you identify this St. Louis Blues draft pick?

    a) Danny Grant
    b) Tony Currie
    c) Al Macadam
    d) Mark Kirton

GAMES

CROSSWORD CLUES

Across

1. Maritime home of international pond hockey tournament
7. International Hockey League, abbrev.
9. In 2001–02, Sidney Crosby played for the Midget ___ Dartmouth Subways
10. Al MacNeil was head coach for this NHL team in 1971 (singular)
12. *Hockey Night __ Canada*
13. Charline Labonté's QMJHL team in 1999–2000
15. _____ *de vivre* (French)
16. Curling's big event
17. Frederictonian breaker of NHL colour barrier Willie _____
20. Doubles tennis star from NB, partner of Nestor
23. 1976 Olympics swimming star Nancy _____

25. Major league pitcher Rheal Cormier was one in Moncton before going pro.
27. The Paris Crew slept with one before their big race.
29. 1968–69 Calder Trophy winner for the Minnesota North Stars Danny _____
30. "Spaceman" ____ once played in the New Brunswick Senior Baseball League.
31. Number of men in Canada's 1998 gold medal-winning bobsleigh
32. Irishtown, NB, softball star _____ Willis
34. _____, myself and I
35. Newfoundland, abbrev.
36. The CFL's Larry Uteck was one

40. "___ shoots! _____ scores!"
41. Canadian NBA star Steve _____
42. Skip of 2006 Olympic gold medal winning men's curling foursome Brad _____

Down

1. Sidney Crosby's NHL home
2. Left-handed, abbrev.
3. 1989 Conn Smythe Trophy winner ____ MacInnis
4. Minnesota Twins reliever who once played for the Saint John Dodgers: Jeff _____
5. Golf queen and Charlottetown native Lori _____
6. Cup awarded to Canadian university football champs
10. TV comedian Drew _____
11. "___ ounce of prevention is worth a pound of cure."
14. The first shot on a golf hole uses one
15. Until 2006, head coach of the UNB women's basketball team _____ Slipp
18. Essential for hockey and figure skating
19. "MC" of Montreal Canadiens, spelled out
21. Former home of the Phoenix Coyotes
22. Boxing's "Fighting Fisherman" Yvon _____
24. In 2005, the __ Canada Cup, awarded to the Canadian Major Midget AAA Champ, had its name changed to the Telus Cup.
25. Mount Allison University, for short
26. "In fighting _____"
27. Hello, in Spanish
28. American Eagle, abbrev.
29. Fifty of these per season equals NHL stardom
32. Winnipeg's former NHL team
33. Nickname for a Halifax Voyageur
35. The National Hockey League
36. Alcoholics Anonymous, for short
37. "_____ my! What a goal!"
38. You, in French
39. It's so Canadian, __?

(Solution on page 89)

GIVE ME THAT STAT!

Number of NL baseball players to win a World Series ring: 1

Number of NL athletes or teams to win an Olympic medal: 1

Number of NS canoeists to win an Olympic medal: 1

Number of NS rowers to win an Olympic medal: 1

Number of AHL franchises in Moncton from 1978–93: 4

Number of AHL franchises in Moncton to win Calder Cup: 1

Number of Atlantic Canadian AHL teams to win Calder Cup: 6

Number of Halifax-based AHL teams to win Calder Cup: 3

Number of NHL franchises to have affiliation with Halifax-based AHL teams: 5

Number of times a Nova Scotian has won the Boston Marathon: 3

Number of Nova Scotians to win the Boston Marathon: 2 (Johnny Miles won twice)

Number of Nova Scotians to play on Stanley Cup-winning teams: 5

Number of NS hockey players to win the World Junior Hockey Championship: 3

Number of leagues Robbie Forbes played in from 1981–86: 4

Number of scoring titles won by Robbie Forbes
from 1981–86: 4

Number of NS NHL players to score 100 career goals or more
in regular season play: 4

Number of times NS has captured the Canadian Men's
Curling Championship (now called the Brier): 3

Number of times a NS team has won the Scott
Tournament of Hearts: 7

Number of NS skips to win the Scott Tournament of Hearts: 2
(Colleen Jones won six times)

Number of Canadian Championships won by Dartmouth, NS,
figure skater Rob McCall and his partner, Tracy Wilson: 7

Number of Olympic medals won by Rob McCall
and Tracy Wilson: 1

Number of teams played on by Sidney Crosby in the three
seasons prior to his rookie NHL season: 7

Number of championships won by Sidney Crosby in the three
seasons prior to his rookie NHL season: 5

Number of times football player Chris Flynn won the Hec
Creighton Trophy for Saint Mary's Huskies: 3

Number of Vanier Cup appearances by Saint Mary's University
Huskies under coach Larry Uteck: 3

Number of current NS-born CIS head football coaches: 1

WHERE DID THEY COME FROM?

Match the following athletes with their home provinces

Brad Richards (hockey)	NB	NL	NS	(PEI)
Brad Gushue (curling)	NB	(NL)	NS	PEI
Lori Kane (golf)	NB	NL	NS	(PEI)
Fabian Joseph (hockey)	NB	NL	NS	PEI
René Duprée (wrestling)	NB	NL	NS	PEI
Ron Turcotte (horse racing)	NB	NL	NS	PEI
Rob McCall (figure skating)	NB	NL	NS	PEI
Marianne Limpert (swimming)	NB	NL	NS	PEI
Rob Butler (baseball)	NB	NL	NS	PEI
Anna Pendergast-Stammberger (basketball)	NB	NL	NS	PEI

ANSWERS: Brad Richards (hockey) PEI, Brad Gushue (curling) NL, Lori Kane (golf) PEI, Fabian Joseph (hockey) NS, René Duprée (wrestling) NS, Ron Turcotte (horse racing) NB, Rob McCall (figure skating) NS, Marianne Limpert (swimming) NB, Rob Butler (baseball) NL, Anna Pendergast-Stammberger (basketball) PEI

ANSWERS

1. a) Boston Bruins

Willie O'Ree made his NHL debut with the Boston Bruins in the winter of 1958. O'Ree, a skilled player noted for his tremendous skating and playmaking ability, did not register a goal or an assist in his first NHL hockey game, but his place in professional sport was secured forever by his appearance in a Bruins uniform that night.

2. b) 1910

At just 5 feet 3 inches and 116 pounds, Fred S. Cameron was hardly an imposing figure as he took his spot in the mass of runners at the beginning of the 1910 Boston Marathon. Relatively obscure before the fourteenth edition of the race, Cameron would become forever famous when he forged ahead of American favourites Henri Renaud and Sam Mellor to take the crown.

3. c) The Paris Crew

To say that the foursome's win at the Paris Regatta of 1867 was a major upset is gross understatement. The British and French owned the sport of rowing in the mid-1800s, and the presence of the club from Saint John was simply seen as a way to round out the race. Not only did the crew win the Paris Regatta, but it also took the 1868 championship of America at Springfield, Massachusetts.

4. d) St. John's, NL

In the early days of Stanley Cup competition, teams from Atlantic Canada were a force on the national hockey scene. From 1900 to 1913, no fewer than four teams from Atlantic Canada (Halifax Crescents, New Glasgow Cubs, Moncton Victories, and Sydney Miners) took on teams from Central Canada for the right to hoist Lord Stanley's Cup.

5. d) seventeen

Unbelievably, *Bluenose* ran undefeated for seventeen consecutive years. Built as both a cod fishing ship and a racer, *Bluenose* defeated the legendary *Elsie* out of Gloucester, Massachusetts, in its first notable race and remained unbeaten until retirement. *Bluenose* has been immortalized on the Canadian ten-cent coin.

6. George Dixon

In 1890, Halifax's George Dixon won the World Bantamweight Championship.

7. Halifax Wolverines, Moncton Hawks, Saint John Beavers, Charlottetown Abbies

8. The Moncton Hawks

The Hawks captured the Allan Cup in back-to-back seasons (1932–33 and 1933–34).

9. Vince Ferguson

Ferguson scored the "Million Dollar Goal" while playing for the 1935 Allan Cup Champion Halifax Wolverines. The goal came in game one of the best-of-three Allan Cup semifinal series against the Montreal Royals. Down 3–2 with two minutes left in the game, Ferguson shot the puck from inside the centre ice line at Montreal goalie Pat Sequin. Just before reaching Sequin, the puck took a bad (and for Halifax, lucky) bounce before finding the back of the net. Halifax went on to win the game, the semifinal series, and eventually the Allan Cup.

10. The Truro Bearcats

While playing for the Midget AAA Dartmouth Subways, Crosby also played three games for the Bearcats of the Maritime Junior A Hockey League during the 2001–2002 regular season. A fourteen-year-old at the time, Crosby did not score any goals in games played against Dartmouth, Halifax and Campbellton.

11. b) The Fighting Fisherman

Yvon "The Fighting Fisherman" Durelle was one of the more feared heavyweight contenders of the 1950s and '60s. A powerful puncher who just never went down no matter how hard he got hit, Durelle came close to winning the World Light-Heavyweight Championship in December of 1958 in a fight against the legendary Archie Moore. Durelle had Moore in trouble early and often in the bout but could not put the American away before succumbing to Moore's fighting prowess in the eleventh round.

12. d) Mr. McKenna defended boxer Yvon Durelle against murder charges

In the late 1970s, famed New Brunswick fighter Yvon Durelle was charged with murder. Frank McKenna, a lawyer based in what was then the town of Chatham, NB (now the city of Miramichi), defended Durelle and won an acquittal for the light heavyweight champion. McKenna would soon move on to provincial politics and was swept to power as the premier of the province in 1987.

13. d) Ted Williams

"Teddy Ballgame" was the greatest hitter the game of baseball has ever known. The last man to hit over .400, batting .406 back in 1941, Williams was a seventeen-time all-star and a Triple Crown winner in 1947. Williams' acumen with the rod and reel is as well documented as his ability with the bat, and he loved to spend time on the Miramichi River fishing the famed Atlantic salmon.

14. b) First black Canadian to sign a major league baseball contract

Jackie Robinson certainly got more press for his heroic breaking of the colour line in baseball than did Manny McIntyre, but all of professional sport should give a tip of the cap to McIntyre for having led the charge north of the border. In 1946, McIntyre signed a professional contract with the Sherbrooke Canadians, the farm club of the St. Louis Cardinals, a monumental feat considering the state of professional baseball and its attitude toward black ballplayers at that time.

15. d) The British Empire Games

In 1930, William Lloyd McIntyre won the very first gold medal at the British Empire Games. At the time of his gold medal performance in Hamilton, McIntyre was recognized as the best wrestler in North America. External circumstances kept McIntyre from competing at the Olympic level, but he would end his career undefeated and was inducted into the PEI Sports Hall of Fame in 1978.

16. The Halifax Atlantics

Gallivan's big break came on New Year's Eve, 1950, when regular announcer Doug Smith fell ill and Gallivan was asked to fill in. By 1952, Gallivan was the full time announcer for the newly established *Hockey Night In Canada*.

17. Connie MacNeill

On February 27, 1950, the Acadia Axemen forward scored three times in six seconds during the second period against the Kentville Wildcats. All three goals were scored in a four-on-four format due to coincidental penalties. The game was played at the old Acadia arena in Wolfville, Nova Scotia.

18. Moe Drabowsky

In the first game of the 1966 World Series featuring Baltimore and Los Angeles, Orioles relief pitcher Drabowsky struck out eleven Dodgers to set a new single game World Series record. He also fanned six consecutive batters to tie a previous record set by Cincinnati Reds pitcher Horace Eller in 1919.

19. Johnny Miles, in 1926 and again in 1929

Miles was born in Halifax, England, but moved to Sydney Mines when he was still a toddler.

20. Ty Cline

In the 1969 major league baseball expansion draft, former Arrow Cline was drafted by the Montreal Expos from the San Francisco Giants. Cline played 101 games in his only season with the Expos.

21. The ballpark was named Little Brooklyn, after Ebbets Field, the famed home of the Brooklyn Dodgers. Razed more than four decades ago, Little Brooklyn sat on the present-day site of the Holiday Inn, next to the Angus L. MacDonald Bridge.

22. c) Pittsburgh Penguins

Despite being the number two goalie in Pittsburgh behind the flashy Tom Barasso, Wendell Young's value to the Pens during their back-to-back championship run was without debate. Young would bring his championship experience to Tampa Bay in 1993–1994 before closing out his impressive career with the IHL's Chicago Wolves in 2001.

23. b) Only one of two Canadians to hit thirty-five or more home runs in a single season.

Perhaps only Larry Walker, the former Colorado Rockies MVP, has put up more impressive numbers for positional players native to Canada than Matt Stairs. In 1999, Stairs topped the thirty-five home run mark as a member of the Oakland Athletics, becoming only the second Canadian in Major League Baseball history to do so. At the end of the 2006 season, Stairs was still bashing baseballs as a member of the Texas Rangers.

24. b) Columbus Blue Jackets

Gerard Gallant was a fierce competitor during his playing days in the NHL. He and linemate Steve Yzerman epitomized the grit and grace that were the trademark of the Red Wings during the late 1980s and early 1990s. Confident of Gallant's ability to bring that fire to his expansion Blue Jackets club, GM Doug MacLean introduced Gallant as the third coach in team history in June of 2004.

25. a) Mount Allison Mounties

From 1995 until his graduation from the Mounties program in 1998, Eric Lapointe was acknowledged as the best running back in the CIS. In 1996, Lapointe set a CIS record by rushing for an amazing 1,169 yards, while in 1998 he led university football with 191 rushes, 1,515 yards and 10 touchdowns. Lapointe would be drafted by the Edmonton Eskimos in 1999 and is entering his eighth season in the pro circuit.

26. c) The Brier

From St. John's, Bob Cole has broadcast professional hockey games for well over three decades. Perhaps Cole is best re-membered for his infamous call "They're going home! They're going home!" after the Russian Red Army team left the Spec-trum ice in Philadelphia during a brutally vicious exhibition game against the Flyers in January of 1976. An all-around athlete, Cole also made a name in national curling circles by representing his home province at the Brier Curling Champion-ship in 1971 and 1975.

27. Chris Clarke

In 1975, while fighting in the 132-pound division, Chris Clarke beat Aaron Pryor to win the gold medal. In his professional career, Pryor went on to win the WBA Welterweight title and in 1996 was inducted into the International Boxing Hall of Fame.

28. Rick Bowness

In 1988–89, Halifax native Bowness was behind the bench for 28 Jets regular season games. In 2004, Bowness served as an interim head coach in Phoenix for the team's last 20 games.

29. Acadia Axemen: 1965, 1971, 1977
    Saint Mary's Huskies: 1973, 1978, 1979, 1999
    St. F. X. X-Men: 1993, 2000, 2001

30. Al MacInnis, 1989 Calgary Flames
    Brad Richards, 2004 Tampa Bay Lightning

While playing for the 1989 Stanley Cup-winning Calgary Flames, defenceman Al MacInnis was named the Conn Smythe winner. The Cape Breton native scored 7 goals while adding 24 assists in the 1989 post-season, leading Calgary to the Stanley Cup.

In 2004, Tampa Bay Lightning forward Brad Richards led the Lightning to its first-ever Stanley Cup. Richards, a Murray Harbour, PEI, native, scored 12 goals to go with 24 assists in 23 playoff games to lead the Lightning to the championship.

31. Steve Sumarah

Halifax native Sumarah was named head coach for the Saint Mary's Huskies in March of 2006. Sumarah had worked the previous twelve years as an assistant football coach in the CIS.

32. b) Campbellton, NB

Gordie Gallant was a feared enforcer for the Minnesota Fighting Saints of the now defunct World Hockey Association in the mid 1970s. In 1972, before his stint in the WHA, Gallant was the main physical presence for this Northern New Brunswick outfit during their Hardy Cup quest.

33. b) 1993 Toronto Blue Jays

One can only imagine how thrilling it must have been for native Canadian Rob Butler to win a World Series with the 1993 Toronto Blue Jays. Butler played in seventeen games for the Jays that season, going an impressive 13 for 48 in a limited utility role. In the post-season Butler would get a couple of at-bats for the Jays, and he made them count by getting a timely hit against the Phillies.

34. a) Stacy Wilson

Moncton, NB, native Stacey Wilson was named the first-ever team captain for Team Canada's Olympic women's hockey team. Wilson, a veteran of numerous world championships, would be selected for the honour based on her exceptional leadership skills and impressive hockey resumé. A decorated member of the national program, Wilson would author a book on hockey following her retirement from the game.

35. d) Edmonton Eskimos

Chris Skinner's timing could not have been better. In 1984, the Edmonton Eskimos were in a rebuilding mode and were looking for a powerful back who could make an immediate impact. Enter Chris Skinner. The Quebec–Ontario Football Conference MVP in 1983 became a mainstay in the Eskies' backfield and led them to a Grey Cup victory in 1987. Skinner would have short stints in Ottawa and Vancouver before calling an end to his impressive career in 1991.

36. d) Moncton Blue Eagles

Jean Perron brought the Moncton Blue Eagles hockey program to the forefront of Canadian university hockey in the early 1980s. In 1981, the Blue Eagles halted the University of Alberta Golden Bears' three-year winning streak with a victory on Alberta's home ice. In 1981–82, Moncton made it back-to-back titles with a thrilling win in front of home fans in Moncton. By 1985, Perron could not resist the lure of the NHL and took over behind the Canadiens' bench, leading them to a Stanley Cup win in May of 1986.

37. 1966: St. Francis Xavier X-Men
    1973: Saint Mary's Huskies
    1979: Acadia Axemen
    1981: Acadia Axemen
    2001: Saint Mary's Huskies
    2002: Saint Mary's Huskies

For the first two years of competition, the championship was an invitational event, with a national panel selecting two teams to play, much like the system employed by American college football today.

38. Paul Boutilier, Sidney Crosby, and Stephen Dixon

Sydney native Boutilier played on the 1982 gold medal-winning Canadian team. He would go on to win a Stanley Cup with the New York Islanders in 1983.

In 2005, Cole Harbour's Crosby and Halifax's Dixon also took home gold medals while playing for Team Canada. The pair also played for Canada's silver medal-winning squad at the 2004 World Junior Hockey Championship.

39. Saint John and Halifax

In 1986, the Montreal Alouettes played the Winnipeg Blue Bombers in Saint John. In 1987, the Alouettes played the Tiger Cats, also in Saint John. In 2005, the Toronto Argonauts played the Hamilton Tiger Cats in pre-season CFL action at Huskies Stadium in Halifax.

40. Don MacAdam

In three seasons at the Charlottetown Civic Centre, the Senators compiled a 102–113–22–3 record.

41. Ray Downey, 1988
      David Defiagbon, 1996

In 1988 at Seoul, Halifax native Downey won a silver medal for Canada while fighting in the light-middleweight division.

In 1996 at Atlanta, David Defiagbon, also from Halifax, was a silver medallist in the heavyweight division.

42. c) Stephenville, NL

There may not be a more passionate corner of the country in terms of its hockey than Newfoundland and Labrador. It was only appropriate then that the town of Stephenville have the honour of hosting *Hockey Day in Canada* in January, 2006. The town, which has been hit by some tough economic times of late, did a sensational job of hosting the day-long event; even premier Danny Williams took time from his busy schedule to play some shinny during the week.

43. d) Montreal Alouettes

Larry Uteck was an outstanding defender in the Canadian Football League. Known as a punishing tackler, Uteck played in the league from 1973 until 1981. In 1978, Uteck joined the Montreal Alouettes and immediately made his presence known, helping the already talented Montreal Club to a Grey Cup appearance against the Edmonton Eskimos.

44. b) Danny Grant

Danny Grant was one of the purest goal scorers in the National Hockey League during his thirteen-year stay in the circuit. In 1974–1975, Grant scored 50 goals in 80 games during his first year with the Detroit Red Wings. One can only wonder how good Grant's NHL numbers might have been had he not played with second division clubs like Detroit and Los Angeles throughout most of his stint in the bigs. Danny Grant did win one Stanley Cup as a member of the 1967–68 Montreal Canadiens.

45. d) Acadie-Bathurst Titan

Charline Labonté played 26 games for the Acadie Bathurst Titan during the 1999–2000 season. Labonté was certainly not just a novelty in the "Q," earning over a thousand minutes of playing time with a very respectable 5.22 goals against average in the offense-oriented CHL circuit. Labonté eventually turned to the national women's program and found herself between the pipes as Canada defended its gold medal against Sweden in the 2006 Olympics.

46. a) Anaheim Angels

In 1997, Jason Dickson of the Anaheim Angels burst onto the professional baseball scene with a spectacular sophomore season. After going 1–4 in his rookie campaign a year earlier, Dickson found his control and deftly used his wide array of pitches to confound opposition batsmen. Injuries would ultimately cut into his effectiveness and he would finish his four-year stint in the bigs with a 26–25 record.

47. John Brophy

Antigonish, NS, native Brophy is second with 1,027 victories. Now retired, Brophy coached in the Eastern, Southern, American, Central, National, and East Coast Hockey Leagues.

48. Karen Moore (née Fraser)

Former Dalhousie Tiger and CIAU All-Canadian Moore played for Canada at the 1984 Summer Olympics in Los Angeles. Canada's women's volleyball team went on to finish eighth at the Olympic tournament.

49. Darren Langdon, Sidney Crosby, Aaron Downey and Eric Boulton

Langdon of the New Jersey Devils played for the Summerside Capitals in 1991–92.

Crosby played three games for Truro during the 2001–2002 regular season.

Montreal Canadiens forward Downey played for the Cole Harbour Colts from 1993–95.

Atlanta Thrashers forward Eric Boulton played for the Cole Harbour Colts from 1993–95.

50. Brett Hull scored fifty goals while adding forty-two assists for the Moncton Golden Flames in 1986–87.

51. Jack MacDuff

In 1976 Newfoundland's MacDuff won the Brier, a first for his home province and through 2006, the only Brier championship for Newfoundland. MacDuff's teammates were Toby McDonald, Doug Hudson and Ken Templeton.

52. b) Columbus Blue Jackets

Some readers familiar with the Columbus connection to PEI may have gotten this one quite easily. Summerside native Doug MacLean was the GM of the Blue Jackets when they made the trek to Summerside just before the 2002–03 campaign. In addition to NHL hockey, the town has been a host venue for numerous national and international championships over the past two decades and has made sporting events a staple of its tourism industry.

53. c) Tampa Bay Devil Rays

Rheal Cormier has ridden a lively left arm to a very successful MLB career for parts of three decades. A sixth-round pick by the Cardinals in 1988, the former Moncton Met evolved into a very effective middle reliever for the Red Sox and Phillies after seeing action as a starter for the Cards. Cormier was a member of Team Canada's pitching staff at the 2006 World Baseball Classic.

54. b) Her participation in the LA Games was the first ever for a female athlete from PEI.

With her participation in the 1984 Summer Olympics in Los Angeles, Anna Pendergast-Stammberger became the first female athlete from Prince Edward Island to participate in an Olympic Games. Stammberger played a key role in Canada's fourth place finish in 1984, playing in every game and earning rave reviews for her play in the paint against much bigger opponents.

55. a) Chicago Blackhawks

Everett Sanipass was once described as having the perfect athletic physique. In 1986, the Chicago Blackhawks, in need of a strong physical presence in their forward unit, took the QMJHL star with their first pick, the fourteenth selection overall. Sanipass would play in parts of four seasons for the club from the "Windy City" before being shipped to the Quebec Nordiques in the 1989–1990 season. The talented left winger would score 59 points in 164 NHL games before calling it quits in 1993.

56. New Jersey Devils

Crosby played in an NHL regular season game for the first time on October 5, 2005, in East Rutherford, New Jersey. The Penguins lost the season opener to the Devils 5–1. Crosby assisted on the only Pittsburgh goal while logging 15:50 in ice time during the game.

57. In 1980–81, while playing for the Charlottetown Eagles, Robbie Forbes led the Island Junior "A" Hockey League in scoring. Two years later, while playing for the Halifax Lions of the Metro Valley Junior 'A' Hockey League, Forbes won another scoring championship. In 1984–85, he played one season for the University of New Brunswick Red Devils, leading the Atlantic Conference. The next season, while playing for the Cornerbrook Royals, Forbes led the Newfoundland Senior League in scoring, capturing his fourth scoring championship in five years.

58. Colleen Jones

Halifax's Jones won the Scott Tournament of Hearts six times: 1982, 1999, 2001, 2002, 2003 and 2004

59. Bobby Smith, Paul MacLean, Al MacInnis, and Sidney Crosby

In 1981–82 Bobby Smith, a native of North Sydney, totaled 114 points for the Minnesota North Stars. (Smith was born in North Sydney, but grew up in Ottawa.)

In 1984–85, Antigonish native Paul MacLean had 101 points for the Winnipeg Jets. (MacLean was born in France, but grew up in Antigonish.)

In 1990–91, Port Hood's Al MacInnis had 103 points for the Calgary Flames.

In 2005–2006, Cole Harbour's Sidney Crosby had 102 points in his rookie season for the Pittsburgh Penguins.

60. Al MacNeil

In 1971, Sydney's Al MacNeil was the head coach for the Stanley Cup champion Montreal Canadiens.

61. New Brunswick Hawks and St. John's Maple Leafs

From 1978–82, the New Brunswick Hawks were the AHL farm team for the Chicago Blackhawks and Toronto Maple Leafs. From 1991–2005, the Toronto Maple Leafs placed their top minor league players in St. John's.

62. d) Mike Eagles

No sitting president of the United States of America had ever attended an NHL playoff game until Bill Clinton accepted an invitation from the Washington Capitals owner during the club's series against the Buffalo Sabres. The president could not have picked a more exciting game as Capital forward Todd Krygier snapped an overtime winner past Sabres keeper Dominik Hasek before a raucous sold-out crowd at the MCI Center.

63. c) Janiva Willis

Janiva Willis was named to the 2004 Canadian Olympic team on the strength of her outstanding play with Winthrop of the NCAA. Her accomplishments include NCAA Woman of the Year for the state of South Carolina, NCAA Woman of the Year Top Ten finalist in the country, 2005 NFCA All-American Scholar Athlete, as well as being the national all-time leader in games played (234), at-bats (711), total runs (174), hits (245), doubles (51), home runs (30), and walks (90).

64. c) 200 metre individual medley

For months leading up to the Summer Olympics in Atlanta, the big debate in the high-profile sport of swimming surrounded the 200 IM and the anticipated battle between Ireland's Michelle Smith and Fredericton's Marianne Limpert. There has always been the suspicion that Smith used performance-enhancing drugs, and the rumour resurfaced following Smith's split-second victory over Limpert in the final. Limpert would participate in three Summer Olympic Games and the 2002 Commonwealth Games, where she finished third in the 200 IM.

65. c) Tracy Wilson and Rob McCall won a bronze medal at the 1988 Calgary Winter Olympics.

66. d) University of New Brunswick

Therese Brisson's impact on the game of women's hockey is often compared to that of American soccer superstar Mia Hamm. A true pioneer in her sport, Brisson was all about passion, pride, and the Canadian way of playing the game. In 2000, under somewhat negative circumstances, Brisson left her job as an assistant professor of kinesiology at UNB in order to continue her pursuit of an Olympic gold medal. Ultimately, Brisson reached her goal as Canada avenged their stunning 1998 final game loss to Team USA by capturing gold at the 2002 Salt Lake City Olympics.

67. In 1983, Sydney-born Paul Boutilier won a Stanley Cup as a defenceman for the New York Islanders.

1986, North Sydney native Bobby Smith helped the Montreal Canadiens win the Stanley Cup.

Smith's teammate was Mike MacPhee from River Bourgeois.

In 1989, when the Calgary Flames captured their first Stanley Cup in franchise history, Port Hood's Al MacInnis played defence for the Flames.

Sydney's Al MacNeil worked in the Calgary Flames' front office.

68. Alf LeJeune from Sydney was an NHL referee from 1972–84.

69. Quarterback Chris Flynn won the award for the Saint Mary's Huskies in 1988, 1989 and 1990. He is the only player to win the Hec Creighton Award three times.

Running back Eric Lapointe from the Mount Allison Mounties won the Hec Creighton twice, in 1996 and 1998.

70. Summerside Western Capitals in 1997; Halifax Oland Exports in 2002.

71. Halifax and Dartmouth

72. b) Don Sweeney

The Boston Bruins of the 1990s were about two stellar defence-men: superstar Ray Bourque and the ultra-steady Don Sweeney. Beginning in the 1988–89 season, Sweeney patrolled the Bruins' blueline with impeccable attention to detail and an un-wavering work ethic that endeared him to a number of bench bosses including Mike Milbury and Pat Burns. Sweeney would play all of his 1,115 games, minus the 63 he played in Dallas, with his beloved Bruins.

73. b) Paul Hodgson became a broadcaster for the CBC.

When Paul Hodgson was signed as an amateur free agent, the Toronto Blue Jays must have felt that at least one of their outfield positions would be solidified for a very long time. Unfortunately for Toronto and for Hodgson, the blue chip prospect from New Brunswick would have to give up the game after only one year in the bigs due to injury. Following his time in the ma-jors, Hodgson spent some time with the CBC as an on-camera personality.

74. d) discus

Clarence Bastarache's performance at the 1973 Pan Am Games was nothing less than inspirational as he took gold in the event despite rumours of a nagging injury. In the 1976 Paralympic Games in Toronto, he won a bronze medal in the pentathlon and helped Canada to a top ten finish. Inducted into the Bathurst Sports Hall of Fame in 1995, Bastarache is also a recipient of the Canadian Paraplegic Association Merit Award.

75. c) New Brunswick

Although women's hockey has made tremendous strides in Atlantic Canada, it has been difficult for regional teams to overthrow powerhouse teams in Alberta, Quebec and Ontario in order to find themselves on the podium at the Esso National Women's Hockey Championship. Only New Brunswick has been able to medal at the national tourney, winning a silver in 1995 and following that effort with a bronze at home in Moncton in 1996.

76. d) Secretariat

Ron Turcotte and Secretariat were money in the bank in 1973. After having won the Kentucky Derby and the Belmont Stakes with a horse named Riva a year earlier, Turcotte took over the reins of Secretariat and helped guide her to the most impressive Kentucky Derby win in the history of the race. Turcotte, the first jockey to win back-to-back Kentucky Derbies since 1902, continued to have huge success on the circuit until his career ended prematurely in 1978 when he broke his sternum and two vertebrae during a race. Turcotte would receive the Order of Canada in 1974 and gained entrance into the Canadian Sports Hall of Fame in 1980.

77. In 1971–72, 1975–76 and 1976–77 the Nova Scotia Voyageurs won Calder Cups. Note: The Vees never won another championship after leaving the Halifax Forum for the downtown confines of the Metro Centre.

In 1981–82, the New Brunswick Hawks became the second Atlantic Canadian franchise to win an AHL championship. In 1992–93, the Cape Breton Oilers captured their first Calder Cup. In 2001, the Saint John Flames won that city's first and only Calder Cup.

78. Outfielder/first baseman/designated hitter Matt Stairs from Fredricton, NB, and left-handed pitcher Rheal Cormier from Shediac, NB.

79. 1. Montreal Canadiens
    2. Atlanta Flames
    3. Edmonton Oilers
    4. Chicago Blackhawks
    5. Quebec Nordiques

The Montreal Canadiens were the primary supplier of minor league talent for the Vees, but in the mid-1970s, the Atlanta Flames also shared the affiliation. One notable player from the Atlanta organization who starred with the Vees was Guy Chouinard. Chouinard had 80 points in 1975–76 for the Voyageurs.

From 1984–88, Edmonton and Chicago shared affiliation with the Nova Scotia Oilers.

From 1989–93 the Halifax Citadels were the AHL farm team of the Quebec Nordiques. Note: The Citadels were the last AHL team to be located in the Halifax market.

80. The Moncton Alpines joined the league in 1995 and was renamed the Wildcats in 1996.

81. Mabel DeWare

DeWare skipped her team to a Canadian title. DeWare's team-mates were Harriet Stratton, Forbis Stevenson and Marjorie Fraser. In 1963 the tournament was dubbed the Diamond D Championship. It was not sponsored by Scott Paper until 1982.

82. c) St. Francis Xavier University

Women's hockey became part of the CIS scene during the 1997–1998 season. As with the men's game, University of Alberta has proven to be a force, with no less than four gold medals during that time. The St F. X. women's program has also done very well, making five appearances and acquitting themselves well every time out. The only other Atlantic Canadian club to reach the championships was Saint Mary's; they've made it to the dance three times.

83. a) national basketball team

Canada's national basketball team circa 1976 was one of the best in the world heading into the 1976 Olympics and it was led by NB great Joyce Slipp. Following the 1976 games, Slipp eventually took her hardcourt experience to UNB where she helped transform the CIS program into one of the most respected in the nation. In a fitting farewell, Slipp's charges hosted the national championships in 2006, finishing the season on a strong note and barely missing the bronze medal.

84. a) Mike Weir

On April 13, 2003, Canadian Mike Weir beat out Tiger Woods, Phil Mickelson and the rest of the field to win the famed Masters golf tournament. At the 1992 Canadian Amateur Tournament in Saint John, however, Weir would have to take a back seat to New Brunswick's Darren Ritchie. Ritchie's superb putting and his ability to stay out of trouble throughout the tournament helped him defeat the current PGA pro by two strokes. Ritchie would also win back-to-back New Brunswick championships in 1996 and 1997.

85. b) Team New Brunswick

In the 1970s and 1980s, women's softball had a profile in Atlantic Canada that often rivalled soccer, basketball and even baseball. Team New Brunswick, behind the awesome pitching of Shediac's Vicky Bastarache, outlasted both Alberta and Ontario to take the gold medal in front of a sold-out hometown crowd in Moncton.

86. b) second

Russ Howard's curling resumé is nothing less than sterling. A two-time Brier and world champion, Howard probably assumed his chances of getting to an Olympics were slim to none before Brad Gushue came calling in 2005. After some initial jockeying, Howard eventually took over the position of second from Mike Adam and played an integral part in the Gushue rink's gold medal effort in Italy.

87. The 1952–53, 1953–54 Halifax Atlantics and the 2005–2006 Saint John Scorpions.

In 1952–1953, the Halifax Atlantics captured the Maritime championship and were also awarded the Alexander Cup by default. The Quebec Senior League was still holding its playoff tournament and was unable to compete for the cup, thus the Alexander Cup went to the Atlantics. The Atlantics also won the Alexander Cup in 1953–54.

In 2005, the Canadian Elite Hockey League was launched and featured teams from Summerside, Saint John, Dartmouth and Sydney—all competing for the Alexander Cup. The Saint John Scorpions swept the Dartmouth Destroyers 4–0 in the best-of-seven league final to bring the Alexander Cup back to the Maritimes for the first time in fifty-three years.

88. In 2006, Newfoundland skip Brad Gushue and his four-some won the men's curling gold medal at the Torino Winter Olympics.

89. e) None of the above.

MacInnis and Richards have won a Memorial Cup for Kitchener and Rimouski respectively, but Crosby did not win the major junior championship. Richards and MacInnis have won a Conn Smythe Trophy, but Sidney's Pens missed the playoffs in his rookie season. Crosby and Richards have donned the double blue of the Oceanic and MacInnis spent his time in the WHL and OHL. While Crosby and MacInnis have broken the 100 point barrier, Richards missed the mark by a mere nine points in 2005–2006.

90. Penny LaRocque

In 1983, LaRocque captured the Scott Tournament of Hearts. Her teammates were Sharon Horne, Cathy Caudle and Pam Sanford.

91. Nancy Garapick

The fourteen-year-old Garapick won bronze medals in the 100 metre and 200 metre backstroke events, becoming the only Canadian to win two individual medals at the 1976 Summer Games.

92. e) None of the above

Through 2006 no Atlantic Canadian team has ever captured the Air Canada/Telus Cup. In 2002, Sidney Crosby and the Dartmouth Subways lost to the Tisdale Trojans in the Air Canada Cup championship final.

93. b) An officiating scandal initially robbed Canadians Jamie Salé and David Pelletier of their gold medal.

When Elizabeth Bouma agreed to take on the role of team leader for the national figure skating team at the 2002 Winter Olympics, she could not have anticipated being in the middle of a scandal that would rock the sport to its very core. A French judge admitted to accepting a bribe that initially robbed Canada's Jamie Salé and David Pelletier of a gold medal. After negative worldwide coverage of the scandal, the powers that be decided to give the duo their proper place atop the gold medal podium.

94. b) La Résistance

In 2003, Moncton's René Duprée, the son of the famous grappler Emile Duprée, teamed up with Sylvain Grenier to form the WWE on RAW tag team La Résistance. A former Canadian bodybuilding champion, Duprée has also fought under the name "The Phenomenal One" and "The French Phenom." A popular draw throughout the United States, Duprée has recently signed a new deal that will keep him with the WWE for quite some time.

95. c) His son was not awarded the league's MVP award.

In 2002, Michel Croteau sued the New Brunswick Amateur Hockey Association after his sixteen-year-old son Steven was denied the league MVP award. Steven Croteau was the leading scorer in the NB "AAA" Hockey League, scoring 45 goals and 42 assists in 27 games, yet he was not deemed the most valuable player in the circuit according to coaches and managers.

96. b) 1991 Canada Winter Games

Charlottetown, PEI, hosted the 1991 Canada Winter Games. The Games, widely regarded as one of the best in the history of the event, broke attendance records at the time and helped make the event one of the most important amateur athletic trials in Canada.

97. Al MacNeil

In 1971, MacNeil was the head coach for the Stanley Cup champion Montreal Canadiens. The next season he was behind the bench when the Nova Scotia Voyageurs captured the Calder Cup.

98. Steve Giles

In 2000, at the Summer Olympics in Sydney, Australia, Giles won bronze in the C1, 1,000 metre event. Giles was born in St. Stephen, NB, but grew up in Lake Echo, NS.

99. Danny Grant

Fredericton native Grant led the Minnesota North Stars in scoring during the 1968–69 season. In doing so, he was the Calder Trophy recipient as the NHL's top rookie.

100. The Shearwater Flyers

On November 25, 1957, six thousand fans packed the Halifax Wanderers Grounds to watch the Flyers beat the Fort William Redskins 27–21. With the win the Flyers completed an undefeated season and became the first Maritime team to win the Canadian Senior Football Championship.

101. Springhill, NS, native Anne Murray

102. a) Reardon was arrested on charges of armed robbery

Jeff Reardon can be mentioned in the same breath as super relievers Rollie Fingers, Bruce Sutter, and Goose Gossage. Beginning with his time with the New York Mets in the late seventies until his retirement from the Yankees organization in the mid-nineties, Reardon could get it done on the mound with a blazing fastball or a mesmerizing curve that would leave hitters mumbling on their way back to the dugout. Life after baseball has not been so kind to the former Saint John Dodger stopper, however; he was charged in December 2005 with committing armed robbery at a jewelry store in Palm Beach Gardens, Florida.

103. c) 2000

Charlottetown golfer Lori Kane broke into the LPGA winners circle with a victory at the Michelob Light Classic. Kane actually began her career in 1996, but as is the custom in professional golf, some dues needed to be paid before she was ready to win an event outright. Kane has been one of the true stars of the circuit and her career winnings of over $6,000,000 are a testament to the fact that Lori is almost always on or near the top of the field.

104. b) Great Big Sea

Hockey fans in the Mile High City went absolutely nuts for the musical stylings of Newfoundland/ Labrador's Great Big Sea, the headline act for that year's NHL All-Star Game at the Pepsi Center in Denver, Colorado. The performance by GBS was nothing short of spectacular as they brought down the house and earned rave reviews.

105. b) Canada joined a list of nations that decided to boycott the 1980 Olympics.

When the former Soviet Union invaded Afghanistan, a number of nations, including Canada and the United States, decided to boycott the 1980 Games. The move was devastating to the Atlantic Canadian athletes who had spent the better part of four years practising and preparing for their opportunity to go for gold in Moscow. The USSR would have its revenge four years later when they boycotted the Summer Games in Los Angeles.

106. d) tennis

Frederic Niemeyer's success on the tennis court goes back to his days as an ace with Middle Tennessee State. Niemeyer was named Canada's Player of the Year in 2002 and played in both the singles and doubles brackets at the 2004 Olympics in Athens, Greece. In March of 2004, Niemeyer made it all the way to #134 on the ranking list and has yet to be beaten when teaming up with fellow Canadian Daniel Nestor.

107. The Halifax Mooseheads

In 2000, the Halifax Mooseheads hosted the Memorial Cup at the Metro Centre. The tournament featured the Mooseheads, Rimouski Oceanic, Barrie Colts and Kootenay Ice. The Oceanic defeated the Colts in the final to capture their first Memorial Cup.

108. Russ Howard (1987 and 1993)

A former Ontario curler and two-time Brier champion while curling for his native province, Howard moved to New Brunswick in 1999 but has not recaptured the Brier for his adopted home province.

109. Sidney Crosby

In 2005–2006, Cole Harbour, Nova Scotia, native Sidney Crosby scored 102 points for the Penguins in his rookie season. An eighteen-year-old, Crosby was 100 days younger than Dale Hawerchuk when he scored 103 points for the Winnipeg Jets in the 1981–82 season.

110. Al MacNeil

In 1980–81, the Sydney native was behind the bench for the Flames, coaching the team to a then franchise record 92 points. MacNeil was the Flames' head coach from 1979–1982. He was also an interim head coach with Calgary in 2002–2003.

111. Robert Mills

The Dartmouth native won a bronze in single sculls at the 1984 Summer Olympics in Los Angeles.

112. d) Moncton Mets

The Moncton Mets of the New Brunswick Baseball League gained immediate publicity the minute they signed Bill "Spaceman" Lee in 1984. The former Boston Red Sox and Montreal Expos hurler drew sell-out crowds whenever he took the mound. Lee's antics often overshadowed his incredible pitching talent, but the ultimate showman never disappointed. Lee would pitch for a number of years with the Mets before returning south of the border in an attempt to run for the US presidency in 1988 as a member of the Rhinoceros Party.

113. c) St. F. X. bench boss Steve Konchalski coached Nash at the 1996 Tournament of the Americas.

St. F. X. Coach Konchalski knows about the work ethic, determination and fierce competitiveness of Steve Nash firsthand. In 1996, Konchalski and Team Canada were vying for a spot in the 1996 Olympics in Atlanta. Nash, a first round pick of the Suns, played sensationally at point guard and barely missed leading Canada to a berth. Brazil would defeat Canada in a must-win third place game and earn the final spot in the Olympics.

114. b) Team Sweden

After failing to win the Canadian Junior Curling Championship in three consecutive tries, Suzanne Gaudet of PEI struck gold in 2001 in St. Catharines, Ontario. Gaudet followed up her national title with a world championship that year, thanks to a hard-fought victory over Matilda Mattsson of Sweden. Gaudet would successfully defend her national title at home in 2002 before jumping ranks and heading to the Scott Tournament of Hearts in 2003.

115. d) UNB

The University of New Brunswick was a poor host back in 1980 when they won the CIS Men's Soccer Championships held in Fredericton that year. While pre-season favourites McGill and Alberta failed in their attempt to win the title, UNB rode great goaltending and a defense-first game plan to win their only CIS Men's Soccer crown.

116. c) Nordic skiing

Milaine Theriault has always been known as a superbly conditioned athlete; it is certainly one of the major reasons she has been able to compete for Canada at three Olympics. Theriault was able to crack the top ten in team relay in 2005 after winning a bronze medal in the pursuit, sprint and 30 km skate at the 2004 Canadian Championships in Charlo, NB.

117. Ted Nolan

Nolan won the Jack Adams Award in 1997–98 with the Buffalo Sabres when he led the team to a 40–30–12 record. The next season, largely due to a sour relationship with Sabres general manager John Muckler, Nolan was not re-signed, despite his success. Subsequently he was out of coaching until joining the Moncton Wildcats in 2005–2006.

118. Conroy Nelson

Berbick knocked out Conroy Nelson to capture the vacant Commonwealth Heavyweight Boxing Championship. At the time he was also the Canadian Heavyweight Champion. Trevor Berbick was a native of Jamaica but made Halifax his home in the late 1970s and early 1980s.

119. Norm Ferguson

Sydney native Ferguson had 54 points in 76 games for the Oakland Seals in 1968–69.

120. Ralph Hollett

After losing a decision on points to Clarke, Halifax's Ralph Hollett won in a TKO over Clarke on November 13, 1980.

121. Cornerbrook Royals, 1986
   Charlottetown Islanders, 1991
   Saint John Vitos, 1992
   Truro Bearcats, 1998

122. c) 1988

It was unheard of: junior curling teams from New Brunswick just did not compete for gold at the National Curling Junior Championships—until the Sullivan rink made its presence felt. An Atlantic Canadian junior team had not reached the final of the tournament in over a decade and a New Brunswick team had not won the event since 1970, but the Jim Sullivan rink turned the trick with a win in Prince Albert, Saskatchewan, in 1987. Sullivan would win the world title a year later, and New Brunswick would soon be competing for national titles at all level in the sport thanks in large part to the efforts of the Sullivan foursome.

123. c) Marc Albert

Marc Albert was one of the premier volleyball players in the world in the late 1980s and early 1990s. It is not a reach to say that Albert could have played for volleyball heavyweights Cuba or the United States. Albert's trademark was his ability to hit the stuffing out of the ball; opponents held their breath when the big man began to drive through the ball on his way to scorching another smash to the floor. A star on the World Volleyball Circuit, Albert received all-star recognition in five international tournaments.

124. c) builder

Leroy Washburn was inducted into the New Brunswick Sports Hall of Fame as a builder in 1988. He may have qualified as both an athlete and especially as an official, having officiated at both the 1978 and 1986 Commonwealth Games and the Montreal Olympics of 1976.

125. b) Super Stock

In front of 90,000 spectators at the Pomona, California, raceway in February 1970, sport history was made as Barrie Poole of Prince Edward Island became the first Canadian ever to win a national United States drag racing meet. The following year, Poole surprised Pomona spectators by winning his second consecutive Winternationals Super Stock championship.

126. a) synchronized swimming

Few elite athletes have been able to equal either Fitzsimmons' success or her longevity. The first and only Prince Edward Island athlete to represent Canada in the sport of synchronized swimming, Carol Moore Fitzsimmons competed for PEI at the Canada Winter Games in 1971 and again in 1979. Fitzsimmons joined the national team in 1980 and won a gold medal with the club in St. Moritz in 1982.

127. Troy Crosby played in goal for the now defunct Verdun Juniors.

128. Robbie Ftorek

In 1970–71, Ftorek starred for the Halifax Atlantics, scoring 23 goals while adding 37 assists. Then, as a head coach, he came back to Halifax, leading the Citadels to a 25–19–4 record in 48 games behind the bench.

129. Don Koharski

Dartmouth's own Koharski worked as a referee for the game between the Tampa Bay Lightning and Pittsburgh Penguins. It was his 1500th NHL game. An NHL on-ice official since 1977, Koharski is the second-longest-serving active NHL referee.

130. Acadie-Bathurst Titan: 1998
Halifax Mooseheads: 2000
Moncton Wildcats: 2006

131. The Saint Mary's Huskies have advanced to the University Cup eight times but have never hoisted the trophy.

132. c) 1988 (Seoul)

Though she was clearly Canada's dominant rhythmic gymnast in the 1980s, Moncton's Lise Gautreau-Robichaud participated in only the Seoul Games. While she struggled somewhat in international contests, Gautreau-Robichaud was superb in national events, taking the junior championships in 1981 and 1982 and the Eastern Canadian Championships in 1980–82 and again in 1984.

133. a) figure skating

Although Jeff Buttle and Emanuel Sandhu capture the vast majority of the attention in this country when it comes to male figure skaters, Shawn Sawyer of Madawaska set the world on notice in 2006. His effort to qualify for the Torino Games was nothing short of brilliant and his skate in Italy in February was exceptionally strong for a first-time Olympian. As Sandhu and Buttle begin their inevitable departure from the scene, look for Sawyer to take his spot as a leading Canadian medal threat.

134. a) "Rowdy" Roddy Piper

Born in Saskatchewan, Piper moved to Moncton as a young man and actually began his informal training for the sport in the "hub city." Famous for his kilt and his bagpipes, Piper was one of the all-time greats, winning a WWF Intercontinental Championship and earning a place in the WWE Hall of Fame in 2005.

135. a) speed skating

Mark Lackie was famous for his superb physical and mental conditioning in a discipline that is as tough as any in the Olympic repertoire. In Albertville in 1992, Lackie combined with fellow short-track specialists Fred Blackburn, Laurent and Michel Daignault and Sylvain Gagnon to win a silver medal for Canada in the 5000 metre relay.

136. b) Team Canada and Team Italy would share the gold medal after posting identical times.

After four demanding runs of the bobsleigh course in Nagano, both teams had times of 3 minutes, 37.24 seconds. This scene had been played out before when German and Italian teams had identical final times in Grenoble in 1968, and the rules had been re-written to accommodate such an event. In 1998, both the Italians and the Canadians would share the gold medal, a first in thirty years for the European club and the first ever for a two-man unit from Canada.

137. d) Mark Fawcett

The two-time Olympian and holder of an incredible fourteen snowboarding World Cup titles was continually trying to raise the ceiling in terms of what "boarders" could do on the hills or moguls. Fawcett was a member of the notorious 1998 Canadian Olympic snowboard team that irked the sometimes overly cautious Olympic committee but thrilled the throngs of fans that sold out the snowboarding venue at Nagano.

138. a) Don Cherry

Perhaps it is the Kingston, Ontario, connection he shares with the band that enticed Don Cherry to join the troubled trio in their "The Darkest One" video. Of course, if you are a hockey fan, you already know the band, the Boys, and the bad boy of broadcasting all have a deep affection for our national sport.

139. d) Plaster Rock, NB

The World Pond Hockey Championship began in 2002 with approximately forty squads representing the Atlantic Provinces and Maine. Today, there are over 120 teams representing every corner of our country as well as numerous other nations. The tournament, which helps local charities, has an attendance figure of over 6,000 and is covered by various media outlets throughout North America.

140. John Brophy

In 1984, the Voyageurs left Halifax to become the AHL's Sherbrooke Canadiens. Brophy did not stay with the organization. Instead, he joined the Toronto Maple Leafs as an assistant coach and was later named head coach in 1987.

141. 2001–2002: Dartmouth Midget AAA Subways
2001–2002: MJAHL Truro Bearcats (three games)
2002–2003: Shattuck St. Mary's Prep School
2003: Team Nova Scotia at the 2003 Canada Winter Games
2004, 2005: Team Canada at IIHF World Junior Hockey Championship
2003–2005: QMJHL's Rimouski Oceanic

In addition to setting numerous records and winning scoring titles, Crosby also proved adept at winning championships. In 2002 he led the Dartmouth Subways to the Atlantic Major Midget title. In 2003, Shattuck St. Mary's, a Minnesota-based high school, won the US National High School Championship. In 2005, Canada won the gold medal at the World Junior Hockey Championship. Also in 2005, the Rimouski Oceanic were crowned champions of the Quebec Major Junior Hockey League and runners-up at the Memorial Cup in London, Ontario.

142. Darryl

While he's also been called "The Next One" and "Sid the Kid," Crosby was nicknamed "Darryl" after scoring eight points in his first QMJHL exhibition game, a reference to Darryl Sittler, who once scored ten points in an NHL game.

143. In 1927, Murray McNeill, along with Al MacInnes, Cliff Torey and Jim Donahoe captured the first MacDonald Brier.

In 1951, Don Oyler, along with teammates George Hanson, Fred Dyke, and Wally Knock led Nova Scotia to its second-ever Brier Championship.

In 2004, Mark Dacey, along with teammates Bruce Lohnes, Rob Harris, Andrew Gibson and Peter Corkum led Nova Scotia to the Nokia Brier.

(Since its inception in 1927, the Brier has operated under four major sponsorships: MacDonald Tobacco from 1927–1979, Labatt Breweries from 1980–2000, and Nokia from 2001–2004. Tim Hortons took over full sponsorship in 2005.)

144. c) Hawaii

Just weeks before the 2003 draft, English, a graduate of Fatima High School in St. John's, began to appear on possible first and second round lists. Ultimately though, English's Canadian background may have come back to haunt him as he was passed over in all rounds of the draft. English is currently playing for Virtus Bologna in Italy.

145. Fabian Joseph

The player from Sydney helped lead Canada to a silver medal in Albertville, France, in 1992. He repeated that performance as captain of the 1994 Olympic team in Lillehammer, Norway—a team that lost in a heartbreaking shootout to Sweden.

146. The Halifax Crescents beat the Canadian National Recreation Club 6–3 in non-sudden-death overtime. The game was played in front of 1,000 fans.

147. The 1983 Moncton Midland Hawks.

148. In 1971, the Charlottetown Islanders hosted the Centennial Cup tournament at the old Charlottetown Forum. The Islanders finished runners-up to the Red Deer Rustlers from the Alberta Junior Hockey League.

149. c) track and field

Bill Mackinnon was an accomplished track and field athlete. Mackinnon, the first and only Island athlete to be invited to compete in the prestigious Telegram Invitational Meet in Toronto, won top prize in his sport at the 1969 Canada Summer Games in Halifax/Dartmouth, Nova Scotia. Also in 1969, Mackinnon took part in the first Canadian Pan Pacific Games in Japan, taking home two gold, one silver and two bronze.

150. b) Tony Currie

Oromocto's Currie played almost 300 NHL games with St. Louis and Vancouver among others. In the 1985–86 season, Currie spent the season in a Fredericton Express uniform scoring a team-leading 35 goals and 45 assists for 70 points. During his sixteen-year career, Currie would spend parts of three seasons with the Express and finish his pro career in Italy in 1990.

Crossword puzzle solution

ACKNOWLEDGEMENTS

The authors would like to thank the following organizations for their assistance:

New Brunswick Sports Hall of Fame
Prince Edward Island Sports Hall of Fame
Nova Scotia Sport Hall of Fame
Saint Mary's Athletics and Recreation Department
Dalhousie Athletics and Recreation Department